HC
WORD OF THE LORD

by
Roberts Liardon

ALBURY PUBLISHING

Unless otherwise indicated, all Scripture quotations are taken from the *King James Version* of the Bible.

Holding To The Word Of The Lord
ISBN 1-88008-980-7

Copyright © 1994 by Roberts Liardon
Ministries
P.O. Box 30710
Laguna Hills, California 92654

Published by ALBURY PUBLISHING
P.O. Box 470406
Tulsa, Oklahoma 74137

CONTENTS

1. When Logic And Faith Collide...........................**5**

2. Don't Ever Let Go — Even In Victory..............**23**

3. Why You Don't Need A "Plan B"......................**35**

Chapter 1

WHEN LOGIC AND FAITH COLLIDE

Picture this. You're sitting in a boat, far out on a lake, miles away from the nearest shore.

Suddenly, you hear the unmistakable voice of God.

"Get out of the boat and walk on the water."

What would you do?

Well, first of all, you'd probably bang yourself on the side of the head a couple of times to make sure you weren't hearing things. But suppose that even after you did that, the voice was still as consistent and as loud as ever before.

"Get out of the boat and walk on the water."

There would be only one thing to do in a situation like that, and that would be to get out of the boat and start walking on the water, just as God's voice was telling you to do.

That's what happened to the Apostle Peter. And when he stepped out of the boat it was, to anybody else who may have been watching, a very illogical and perhaps even silly thing to do.

But as long as Peter was responding in faith,

the water might as well have been solid ground. It supported his body without a bit of trouble. However, as soon as Peter let go of God's Word, and began to look at what he was doing from a logical perspective, he was in big trouble. He began to sink like he was wearing concrete boots.

I don't think it's likely that God is going to tell you to go walking across the nearest lake. But then again, He might. But whatever He calls you to do, there are bound to be times when His Word is going to collide with the world's notion of logic and good sense. Other people will tell you that you're foolish if you follow the Word of the Lord. Your own brain may tell you that you're foolish if you follow the Word of the Lord.

But you're never foolish to hold to God's Word. Never in a billion years can you make a wrong move by doing what He tells you to do.

The truth is that when "logic" collides with a direct Word from God, logic crumbles into little pieces, while the Word remains unbroken and unmoved.

The Bible is full of examples of people who were willing to follow God's Word instead of logic and who were blessed beyond measure because of it.

For example:

It was not logical for a humble shepherd named Moses to go before the mighty Pharaoh and demand that he set the Children of Israel free. But that's what God told him to do, that's what he did, and because of it the Israelites were able to leave Egypt and make their way to the Promised Land.

It wasn't logical for Noah to build a huge boat so far from the nearest ocean, but he was obeying God's Word when he did it, and as a result Noah and his family were the only survivors of a world-wide calamity.

It wasn't logical for Gideon to go up against the entire fury of the Midianite Army with a tiny group of men armed with nothing more than pitchers and trumpets, but he did what the Word of the Lord had commanded, and as a result, the nation of Israel threw off its oppressors and gained its independence.

Nor was it logical for Abraham to believe it when God pronounced him to be the father of many nations. After all, he didn't have any children at all, and he and his wife, Sarah, were past the age of child-bearing. Abraham could have looked around himself, shook his head and said, "Lord, you must have me mixed up with somebody else." But he didn't do that, and he did indeed become the father of many nations, just as God had promised he would.

For it was through the lineage of Abraham that Jesus Christ came into the world in the flesh — and so all of us who have surrendered our lives to Christ can consider ourselves to be sons and daughters of Abraham.

Abraham is a great example of someone who believed God's Word in spite of what his natural mind told him.

As Romans 4:3 says, *"Abraham believed God, and it was accounted to him for right-eousness."*

And then, verses 16-21 tell us: *"Therefore it is of faith that it might be according to grace, so that the promise might be sure to all the seed, not only to those who are of the law, but also to those who are of the faith of Abraham, who is the father of us all (as it is written, 'I have made you a father of many nations') in the presence of Him whom he believed, even God, who gives life to the dead and calls those things which do not exist as though they did; who, contrary to hope, in hope believed, so that he became the father of many nations, according to what was spoken, 'So shall your descendants be.'*

"And not being weak in faith, he did not consider his own body, already dead (since he was about a hundred years old), and the dead-ness of Sarah's womb.

"He did not waver at the promise of God through unbelief, but was strengthened in faith, giving glory to God, and being fully convinced that what He had promised He was also able to perform."

Now God may be speaking to you about

something, just the way He spoke to Abraham, but you're struggling to trust God's word in the midst of a different kind of reality you see all around you. I have seen the struggle that some people go through.

For example, when I was still a young boy, the Lord told me that He was going to send me to the nations to preach for Him.

My logical mind said, "What's this about going around the world for God? You don't even have a car! And even if you did, you couldn't afford enough gas to get to the other side of town — much less going to the other side of the world."

But in spite of the doubts that assailed me, I clung fast to the Word of the Lord. I got a map of the world, put it up on my wall, and every morning when I got up to get ready for school, I would hit that map and say, "I'm coming to you, open up!" I kept saying that day after day after day...even though some days my head would tell me that I was crazy. And you know what? God has taken me all over the world, to more than 60 countries, to proclaim salvation through the name and the blood of Jesus Christ!

I'll tell you something else. At first, it wasn't easy for me to get used to doing so much traveling. If I had my own way, I would probably just as soon have stayed home where I was comfortable. Traveling can be very hard on the human body, especially when you're always moving back and forth across time zones. You have jet lag. Sometimes you can't remember what day it is, much less what time it is. It seems like you're always standing in lines, looking for your luggage, and trying to get used to the local food and the local customs.

I was always so glad when I got back home to the United States where I could drink the water right out of the tap without worrying about getting sick, and where I could flip a switch and have electric lights any time of the day or night.

I loved having a chance to see the people in other countries and tell them about Jesus, but the traveling itself could really be exhausting.

After awhile, though, it wasn't so bad anymore. For one thing, as I traveled around the world, I was beginning to see the harvests come in from the seeds I had planted. And that was exciting. For another thing, the desire to preach the Gospel is so strong in me that if I wasn't out there on the road, I would begin to feel antsy and unfulfilled — as if I really wasn't doing what God had called me to do.

And then He spoke to me again.

"Roberts, I want you to build a school for my glory."

"But Lord," my mind protested, "I'm spending so much time on the road. How in the world could I ever build a school for you?"

But the Lord's voice was persistent, and I

knew I would obey — had to obey. As He commanded, I would build a Bible School, where young men and women would be taught how to be effective ministers of the Gospel. It meant an entirely new direction for me. It meant I couldn't travel as much. It felt strange at first, but then came the peaceful assurance that always accompanies obedience.

Has God spoken a specific thing for you to do? Perhaps He has given you something that may not even be in the same ball park with what you are doing right now. You might even be scratching your head and saying, "Well, I sure don't see how that's going to happen."

But you don't have to see how it's going to happen. You just have to trust the Lord, know that His Word is always true, and that what He has proclaimed for you will come to pass if you are obedient and yielded to Him.

Another thing to keep in mind is that you cannot know how God is going to work things out. You can't tell Him, "Well, God, this is how I want You to do it." You must be yielded to Him and not the other way around.

God is not a cosmic errand boy who jumps when we call His name — but He is a loving Father who wants only the best for us, and Who is able to mold us into what He wants us to be.

And it's truly amazing what God can do in the lives of those who really believe His Word.

Several years ago, I read a true story written by the mother of a little boy who was in the third grade. Well, this mom was listening to her son say his prayers one night and was shocked to hear him say, "And thank you Lord, that you're going to let me fly."

When the woman questioned her little boy about his prayer, he said that he was certain that God had spoken to him and told him that he was going to be able to fly.

"You mean on a big airplane, like when we go to see your Grandpa?"

"No, like this." And the little guy began flapping his arms like a bird.

Well, naturally the woman didn't know what to do. After all, little boys <u>can't</u> fly by flapping their arms. But she had worked so hard to build up her son's faith, and she didn't want to do or say anything that might damage it.

In the weeks that followed, he kept on believing that he was going to be able to flap his wings and fly around the room. His faith never wavered.

And then one day, the little boy came home from school all excited. It seems his class was going to put on a performance of Peter Pan, and he had been selected for the starring role!

When the day of the performance came, guess what? The school had rigged up a contraption, consisting of ropes and pulleys, whereby Peter Pan was able to "fly" around the room — and of course he was absolutely beside himself with delight.

As soon as the performance was over, he couldn't wait to run into his mother's arms and say, "See, I told you God said He was going to let me fly!"

Now you may be thinking that it's a very long way from that fulfillment of God's Word to the fulfillment of what He has spoken to you. But is it, really? A little boy believed that God would let him fly around the room and he <u>did</u> fly around the room. Perhaps God has been calling you to do something great for His kingdom, and you look around you and say, "How, Lord? I can't do something like that?" Oh, yes, you can. If you accept and believe God's Word with the faith of a child, you will see the glory of the Lord!

Remember the words of Jesus: "Assuredly, I say to you, unless you are converted and become as little children, you will by no means enter the kingdom of heaven." (Matthew 18:3)

What did Abraham do when God spoke to him? He began to speak the same language that God was speaking. He agreed with God that what He had said was true — that, "Yes, Lord, I believe that I will be the father of many nations.

When God speaks to you, your language must begin to echo God's language. When Abraham first began to say, "I am the father of many nations," I'm sure his friends and neighbors must have thought he was totally out of his mind. Can't you picture them pointing at him and laughing behind his back? "Poor old guy has really lost his mind. Doesn't even have one child and thinks he's the father of many nations."

But Abraham let them laugh. He didn't know how the Word of the Lord was going to be fulfilled. He just knew that it was going to happen!

There are plenty of people in this world who like nothing better than to run around with pins, popping other people's balloons. They don't want God's word to come true. They don't want you to succeed. But don't listen to them. Listen to God!

It's easy to hold onto God's Word when everyone around you agrees with it. It's not so easy when they are vehement in their opposition to it.

When I was still in my teens, God called me into the ministry. He wasn't telling me that He wanted me to go into the ministry "some day." He was telling me that He wanted me to start preaching "right now."

Well, not everybody was thrilled with the idea of a boy-preacher. I heard comments like, "You're too young to be a preacher," and "Are you sure you're really listening to God?" Some people thought I was being presumptuous or that I was getting carried away with a sense of my own importance. They wanted me to know my place and to stay there — to do the things "normal" teenagers do.

But it didn't matter what anyone else said. Even at that early age I knew that God's voice was the only one really worth listening to. And so I began preaching in churches throughout my hometown of Tulsa, and, as a result of my obedience to God's word, I saw hundreds of people come to salvation through faith in Christ.

Unfortunately, this world of ours is full of critics. Do you know what a critic is? That's someone who can't or won't try to do anything himself, but who gets great delight out of criticizing others who <u>do</u> try to do things.

The critic says, "This guy's not much of a teacher," but he won't volunteer to teach himself.

The critic says, "Can you believe she had the nerve to sing a solo in church with <u>her</u> voice?" But she's not about to get up and use her own voice to glorify God.

The critic says, "This fellow's got a lot of nerve, thinking that God has told him to start a Bible school." But he doesn't take the time to listen to what God might be saying to him.

Some people are quick to see the negative in every situation. You give them some good news and they will say, "Yes, but." That's their favorite saying, "Yes, but." "Yes, but what about this?" "Yes, but have you thought about that?" "Yes, but what if such-and-such happens?" Sometimes I have just had to look somebody like that right in the eye and say, "Oh, shut up, in Jesus name!" I'm so happy and so excited when God speaks to me that I can scarcely contain my joy, but then some of my friends start with, "Well, Roberts, what about this, or that?" And that's terribly disappointing, because I didn't ask for a dissecting of the word of the Lord. I wanted my friends to be excited with me regarding what God was going to be doing in my life!

Abraham didn't ask God to give him two chapters of explanation as to how it was going to be possible for him and Sarah to have a child at their advanced age. He just believed God and agreed that "I am the father of many nations." He didn't look at Sarah and say, "No way!" Sarah didn't look at him and say, "That's right...no way!" Abraham and Sarah considered and held fast to what God had said to them.

As Romans 4:20-21 says, *"He did not waver at the promise of God through unbelief, but was strengthened in faith, giving glory to God, and being fully convinced that what He had promised He was also able to perform."*

What does it mean to be fully convinced? I like what Oral Roberts says: "It means that you know that you know, that you know that you know, that you know that you know, that you know that you know, that you know that

16

you know it's so." And that's the way it was for Abraham.

As I said, the world is full of critics and nay-sayers, but what you have to keep in mind is that if God has told you to do something or other, then He knows that you have the ability and the resources to do it. And you can also be assured that He will work through you to accomplish His purposes in your life.

Are people criticizing you and saying nega-tive things about you because you are holding fast to God's Word? Well, just listen to what critics have said about some other people you've probably heard of.

Early in her career, a movie producer told Lucille Ball that she had absolutely no acting talent and that she ought to forget about being in show business. She didn't listen, and all of us who have laughed at her antics are very glad she didn't.

A publishing company sent a letter to a beginning author by the name of Zane Grey saying that he couldn't write, would never be able to write, and that they wished he would stop wasting their time with his material. But Grey kept on writing, and wound up with lit-erally dozens of best-sellers and millions of books sold.

Thomas Edison's father believed his son to be "a dunce," and once whipped the boy in public for his failures at school.

When Ludwig von Beethoven was a boy, his

piano teacher pronounced him as "hopeless," and said that he had no musical ability whatsoever.

I could go on with page after page of examples of people who refused to listen to their critics, but who, instead, continued to pursue their dreams. I am not saying that all of the people I've listed were particularly godly, or that they were following what God had told them to do. I don't know about that one way or the other. But I do know that they didn't listen to their critics and neither should you — especially when God is on your side!

Romans 10:17 tells us that *"faith comes by hearing, and hearing by the word of God."*

Listen to God's word to you, and not to the words of the critics and the nay-sayers, and your faith will be built up to the point where you can see past the barriers and the obstacles that might otherwise keep you from finishing the work that God has called you to.

Faith causes things to happen! Abraham was not weak in faith. He kept rehearsing what God had said — kept on holding to it. He could have focused on the negatives: "I'm an old man. Sarah is an old woman. We've been married all these years without having any children, so how in the world can I believe I'm going to have a son now?"

But instead, he kept focusing on God's

word to him: "You will be the father of many nations."

I am always surprised by how many people in the modern world try to tell God what to think and how to act. Our society is full of people trying to act like Jehovah. When you begin to obey, that's when they start to criticize. "Well, I just don't think you ought to do that?" Those people need to think less and believe and obey more. The Bible says that Abraham held to faith, not being weak in faith. He built himself up. He considered not his body, now dead. He lived in faith that what God had said to him would come to pass, no matter how impossible it may have looked to those who were seeing only through physical eyes.

Always remember that your security is in the word of God. There is no security in how much money you have, or in the fact that you live in a fancy home in a nice neighborhood. There is no security in your career, or the investments you've made. There is not even any security in the relationships you have with other people.

Your money may be stolen, your house may burn down, you may lose your job, and your investments may go sour. Even your friends and loved ones may disappoint you.

Security is found only one place in this world, and that is in the abiding Word of God.

I don't mean to imply that God's word

won't be challenging. It may shake you out of your routine. But it is still true that following and obeying is the only possible source of security.

You know, in the charismatic movement, some people have got to the point where they believe that God only speaks to us in nice, sweet little encouraging words. He says things like, "Oh, my people, I love you. Hang in there and everything will be all right. I know that life can be hard sometimes, but remember that I love you and it will help you get through."

Well, I'm not doubting God's love for a moment, and I do believe that He wants us all to be encouraged and strengthened by His presence in our lives. But I know that He is also calling us to boldness and action in His behalf.

He says things like, "I want you to build a big church for me?"

"Who, me!"

"Yes, you."

"Oh...uh...well, I thought God was talking to me, but I realized now that it must have been the devil. After all, God only says things like, 'Be encouraged. Be at peace. I love you.'"

The God we serve is not like that.

He says things like, "I want you to go and preach the Gospel." "I want you to go and feed the poor in my name." "I want you to get involved in a crisis pregnancy center where you can help save lives." "I want you to become a missionary."

But some of us answer, "What? Me? Oh, well, listen, Lord, you must not know me very well! I can't start a church for you! Why, I can hardly pay my light bill. My children are all in rebellion. My life is so mixed up and confused, please don't ask me to do something great for you!"

Well, let me tell you, if God didn't see in you the ability and capacity to do great things for Him, then He wouldn't *ask* you to do those things. He knows the greatness that He has built into you, and He wants to work with and through you to develop and utilize it.

What is God saying to you?

Whatever it is, believe it, act upon it, and just watch what happens!

Chapter 2

DON'T EVER LET GO — EVEN IN VICTORY

At the beginning of this book, we talked about what happened when the Apostle Peter got out of a boat and started trying to walk on the water. You remember that Peter became distracted by the wind and the waves, momentarily lost his faith, and began to sink like a rock. That moment was undoubtedly etched in Peter's mind forever as one of his biggest failures.

But actually, it began as one of his greatest successes. Peter was doing what no other man has ever done (with the exception of Jesus). He was walking along on the top of the Sea of Galilee like somebody out for a stroll on a Sunday afternoon. Imagine how the other apostles felt when they saw Peter get out of that boat and start walking.

"Look at him, he's actually walking on the water? Can you believe it?"

I'm sure they were thrilled and amazed by their brother's demonstration of faith.

But that's not where the story ended. In his moment of victory, Peter let go of God's Word, and his moment of triumph was swallowed up by failure. I have seen that sort of thing happen so many times.

Sometimes people let go of God's Word because they are surprised by the success that has come their way. They think, like Peter did, "I can't really be doing this! Something's bound to go wrong. I know it's all going to fall apart." And when their fears become stronger than their faith, it does fall apart.

Other people have let go of God's Word because they have become overly confident. They've built up some kind of personal empire, it seems to be running well, and they get to the point where they no longer think they need to listen to God. God may even be telling them that it's time to move on in an entirely new direction, but they're not listening. Instead, they're doing the same old thing, only now they're trying to do it in their own power instead of in God's power, and that always means disaster.

Some people tend to look at God in the same way a child would look at a parent who was teaching him how to ride a two-wheel bicycle. You've seen that, I'm sure. Dad's running along behind his little boy, who's trying his best to keep the handlebars steady <u>and</u> pedal at the same time. Finally, dad gives a big push and the youngster is off, riding on his own. "Thanks, dad, but I don't need your help anymore!"

We can never say, "Thanks, God, but we don't need your help anymore. We <u>always</u>

need His help!

As long as you and I are living on this fallen planet, we are going to face challenges and hurdles. Satan is never going to stop trying to do something to get us to stumble, so there's never a time when it's okay to let go of God's word or His hand.

Sometimes the Lord may tell you to do something that seems totally contradictory to everything else He has asked you to do. If He does this, though, there are at least a couple of things to keep in mind. The first is that the Lord is the only One Who knows how things are going to come together in your life. He is the only One Who sees the twists and turns that will be necessary to get you to where you want to be — to where He wants you to be. The second reason is that God may be wanting to purify your motives. In other words, He wants to ensure that you are holding to His word because you believe and trust Him no matter what, and not because you are looking for the things He can give you.

To explain what I'm talking about, let's go back to Abraham and Isaac. We've already talked about the fact that Abraham believed God's promise that he would become the father of many nations, even though he and his wife were both old and had no children. And so, true to the Word of the Lord, Sarah conceived and gave birth to a son, Isaac.

Now I hope that when Isaac was born, Abraham and Sarah threw a huge party to celebrate, and I hope they invited all of the people who had said, "Abraham, you're crazy to go around saying that God told you you'd be the father of many nations. You must be delirious. God hasn't spoken to you."

I'm sure it would have given Abraham a great deal of satisfaction to show off his baby boy and say things like, "Would you like to hold my delusion for awhile? Hey, you who ridiculed me the most, how'd you like to change his diapers?" How good it must have been for Abraham to be able to say, "See what God can do! He is always true to His word!"

And then what happened?

God said, "Abraham, I want you to go out into the wilderness to offer me a sacrifice — and I want the sacrifice to be your son, Isaac."

Imagine how Abraham must have felt when he heard those words. He had waited so long for this little boy to be born. He had held onto God's promise that he would become the father of many nations, even when his friends and neighbors were laughing at him. And now, as a very old man, he was experiencing for the very first time the joy of a developing father-son relationship. He was discovering what a wonderful feeling parental love can be.

And God said, "I want you to show Me how much you love Me by giving Me the life of your only son."

What would you have done if you were Abraham? Most of us would probably throw what my mother used to call a "conniption" fit.

"What are you talking about, Lord? How can you ask me to do something like this? All of my friends thought I was a nut for believing me when you said I was going to be a father, and now they're really going to think I'm a nut if I offer him up as a sacrifice. I just can't do it! I *won't* do it!"

You see, Abraham had attained his goal. He had become a father. But here came the next challenge, a test to see whether he was willing to sacrifice everything in order to obey God.

And Hebrews 11:17-19 tells us: *"By faith, Abraham, when he was tested, offered up Isaac, and he who had received the promises offered up his only begotten son, of whom it was said, 'In Isaac your seed shall be called,' accounting that God was able to raise him up, even from the dead...."*

Abraham walked out of his home that morning, on his way to sacrifice to the Lord. His servants were with him, Isaac was with him, but there wasn't anything else for a sacrifice. No ram or goat or bull. Picture little Isaac running on ahead of everyone...doing the things little boys do — throwing rocks, kicking at sticks and leaves, and asking a hundred questions. Questions like, "Dad...what are we going to sacrifice?"

And Abraham answers softly, "It's okay son. We'll find something to sacrifice. God will provide." Yet he knows all the while that his precious little boy is going to be placed upon that altar.

He would not be dissuaded from holding fast to the word of the Lord, nor from his faith that God always knew what was right and best. If God said, "I want you to give me your son," then Abraham was going to give God his son. It was that simple.

And so this little procession arrives at the spot where the sacrifice is to take place. Abraham piles the wood on top of the altar and makes other preparations for the sacrifice. But little Isaac is looking around, more perplexed than ever.

"I don't understand, Dad. We don't have any animals with us."

And Abraham is forced to say, "My son, you are the sacrifice."

And having said that, he ties the little boy up, places him on the altar, and prepares to strike him dead. But it is precisely at that moment, and not a moment sooner, that an angel stops Abraham, and tells him that God does not want him to offer the boy as a sacrifice, but was only testing his faithfulness.

But you see, Abraham didn't know that was going to happen. When he raised his knife to strike his son, he didn't understand why this was what God commanded, but he was willing to do it anyway. And he was still believing God's promise that he would be the father of many nations. In the natural, there was no way for Abraham to fit all of the pieces together. They just did not make sense. But Abraham was willing to say, "Lord, I don't understand it. But you do. And I can't do anything other than trust you."

You see, similar things will happen in your life. There will be challenges and oppositions to you. It will look like if you do the things God is telling you to do that everything will be destroyed instead of built up. Persecutions and accusations will come along to make you withdraw from the word, to keep you from being strong in the faith. You will be hit in your spirit to make you let go of the word and hold onto natural things. But if you let go of God's Word, you will die!

I have held onto what God has said to me and have not let go of it. I've been hit, and I've had victories. I have learned that whatever seems to be happening, whether it is good or bad, the most important thing I can do is to hold onto God's Word. It is my foundation, and it is my security!

"Roberts do you know what you're doing?"

"Yes, I'm doing what God has told me to do."

"But, I mean, do you understand what the outcome of this will be?"

"No, I don't need to understand that. All I need to know is that God told me to do it, and He expects me to obey."

Obedience, and not our own understanding, is the key.

It's not as important for me to understand <u>why</u> God wants me to do something as it is important for me to know <u>what</u> He is telling

29

me to do, and be willing to do it.

As we can see from the life of Abraham, it is not always easy to hold to the Word of the Lord. It can be terribly, terribly difficult. In fact, the Bible has many accounts of people who tried to run away from God's Word — but who ultimately found their destinies in obedience.

For example, Moses didn't want to obey when God told him that he had been chosen to bring the Children of Israel out of Egypt. He said something like this: "But Lord, you know how tongue-tied I get. I'll get in front of Pharaoh and start stammering and stuttering and make a complete fool of myself. I really don't think that will convince him that I'm a representative of the One Who created the universe."

But eventually, Moses agreed to do things God's way, and he became the great leader of an entire nation.

When the Word of God came to a young man named Saul, telling him that he had been chosen to be the first king of Israel, Saul tried to hide among some baggage.

He was thinking something like, "What? Me, be king? God...you must have me mixed up with somebody else. I don't want the job. Please...I'm not qualified!"

But God would not be dissuaded from his choice of Saul, and he went on to lead Israel into a number of great military victories.

When God told Gideon that he had been

chosen to lead the Israelites into battle against their oppressors, the Midianites, Gideon replied that he couldn't do it because he came from the least of the families of Israel, and that he was the least one in that least family. But God knew who he was choosing, and Gideon went on to prove on the battlefield that God's choice was the correct one.

There are other examples: Jonah, who tried to run in the opposite direction when God told him to go preach to the people who lived in Nineveh. Jeremiah, who said he couldn't speak to the people because he was only a youth. Elijah, who fled into the wilderness and hid because he thought he was the only one left who was on God's side.

Take a closer look at the lives of some of these heroes from the Bible, though, and you'll find out that they stumbled not at the beginning of their walk with the Lord...but much later on, when they had gained a bit more confidence, when they were flush with the heady feeling of success.

For example, it wasn't until Moses struck a rock to get water for the people, instead of speaking to the rock as God had commanded him to do, that he got into trouble. It seemed natural to Moses to strike the rock, because he had done that so many times before. But this time, God had said clearly to speak to the rock and the water would pour forth. Moses wasn't listening, and he did the wrong thing. As a result, he was not allowed to enter the Promised Land. (See Numbers 20:8-12)

The same thing happened with Saul. God ordered him to destroy all of the Amalekites, but he didn't listen, and as a result the kingdom was taken away from him and given to David. (See 1 Samuel 10:15-28)

And look at Gideon. Fresh from his victory on the battlefield, he fashioned an idol, which "became a snare to Gideon and to his house." (Judges 8:22-28)

Note again that it wasn't in the beginning that these people stumbled. It was when they were gaining confidence. When they were feeling pretty good about themselves, like perhaps they didn't need to listen all that closely to the word of the Lord anymore.

There is nobody anywhere who doesn't *need* to listen to the word of the Lord. There are a lot of people who *aren't* listening to what God has to say, and that's why the world is in such a mess. Remember the old commercial, "When E.F. Hutton speaks, everybody listens." Wouldn't this world of ours be a wonderful place if it were true that when God spoke, everyone listened?

Well, it's not going to happen this side of the Millennium. But it can happen on a personal level — in your life. There is peace, prosperity and joy in the word of the Lord. As Deuteronomy 8:3 says, *"Man shall not live by bread alone; but man lives by every word that proceeds from the mouth of the Lord."* So make a decision that you will hold tightly to God's word for you. That is a decision you will never regret!

Chapter 3

WHY YOU DON'T NEED A "PLAN B"

Let's go back, one more time, to Peter, sitting in that boat on the Sea of Galilee.

He looks up and sees Jesus walking toward him, coming right over the top of the water.

"Lord," he says, "if it's You, let me get out of the boat and walk to You."

And Jesus replies simply, "Come."

What did Peter do? He immediately climbed out of the boat and started walking on the water, heading towards Jesus. Admittedly, he didn't get very far. The Bible tells us that this event took place on a very windy night, and that it was the wind and the waves that took Peter's attention away from his Lord and caused him to begin to sink. But again, what ended up as a rather spectacular failure started out to be a spectacular triumph of faith. For a while, Peter was dancing over those waves like there was nothing to it.

I think we have to admire Peter for having the faith and the courage to get out of the boat in the first place. And I also think we should admire him for the speed with which he followed his Lord's command to "come."

Peter didn't spend a moment trying to put together an alternative plan.

He didn't say, "Er...okay, Lord, I'll be right there. But just in case it doesn't work, let me look around here and see if I can find a flotation device." He didn't even turn to the other disciples and say, "Okay, guys, I'm going to get out of this boat and try to walk on the water. But if it doesn't work, I want you all to be ready to haul me back in here."

No...Peter just got out of that boat and started moving across the water.

I'm afraid that far too many people today are only half-hearted in their obedience to the word of God. They say, "Okay, Lord, I hear you, and I'm willing to follow. But just the same, I think I'd better have a couple of alternatives in mind, in the event that what You have planned for me doesn't work out."

Such thinking shows a complete lack of understanding of the power and faithfulness of God. It can only lead to trouble.

For example, consider what happened between Abraham and Sarah. Sarah thought that a "Plan B" was necessary to fulfill God's promise to her husband.

The Bible doesn't give us a word-for-word description of her conversation with Abraham, but I'm sure it went something like this:

"Look, Abraham...we both know that God has promised to make you the father of many nations. But we also know that I'm well past the time when I can have a baby. But Hagar, my hand-maiden...now there's a woman who is still in the prime of life. *She* could be the one to have your baby. I really think you should think seriously about that."

Now Abraham, like millions of other husbands before and since his day, was willing to do just about anything his wife wanted him to do...so he went in and slept with Hagar, the result being that she became pregnant, and gave birth to a son whom she named Ishmael.

Now, God's promise was to Abraham *and* Sarah. It was not necessary to help God out. There was no need to put a Plan B into place, and the whole thing backfired terribly. First of all, the situation led to strife between Sarah and Hagar — and then between Ishmael and Isaac.

And that strife has continued for centuries. For it was through Isaac that the Jewish race descended, and through Ishmael that the Arab nation was born. Certainly, it was Sarah's (and Abraham's) rashness in believing that they had to help God out by devising a Plan B that has led to centuries of trouble.

You may remember another time when someone thought there was a need for a Plan B — and it resulted in a whole bunch of trouble. That someone was Aaron, the brother of

Moses. I'm sure you remember the story. Moses had gone up on the mountain to receive instruction from the Lord — including the Ten Commandments. In his absence, the people of Israel grew impatient. They didn't know if Moses was coming back. They were tired of following after an "invisible" God. They wanted something they could see, and touch.

And so Aaron gathered up all the gold from the people, melted it down, fashioned it into the shape of a calf, and presented it to them as the God who had brought them out of Egypt.

Such blasphemy! They had seen the plagues which God had brought upon the nation of Egypt. They had seen Him part the Red Sea so they could pass through it, and then bring the waves crashing down on the heads of the Egyptians who tried to pursue them. They had seen the pillar of fire by night and the cloud of smoke by day, leading them the way to the Promised Land, but still, they were ready to trade the glory of the living God for a statue of a cow! Talk about trading a glorious Plan A for a pathetic Plan B. And, of course, the results were disastrous.

There is simply no need, in the world of faith, to have Plan B in your back pocket, because Plan A always works. The most important thing is to spend enough time in prayer and meditation so that you have a clear understanding of Plan A.

Again, I admit that it isn't always easy to follow God's plan for your life. There will be times when, from a natural perspective, it may be downright scary. But you've got to keep your eyes focused on Jesus instead of on the wind and the waves.

For example one year I held a big convention in Minneapolis, Minnesota. At the beginning I really worried, because we had so many big-name speakers coming in, that our expenses were going to run more than $100,000 for the week. If that sounds like a lot of money to you, well it sounds like a lot of money to me, too. And in my soul, I kept dealing with the fear: "What if nobody comes? What are we going to do if we can't pay our bills? What if I'm being presumptuous or foolish?"

Now, I knew in my spirit that I was doing exactly what God had told me to do. So deep down inside of me, I knew that there wouldn't be any problem bringing in enough money to pay the bills and bless the ministries of the speakers who had been asked to participate in the convention. But I really had to cling to the word of the Lord in that regard, because the soul and the flesh were fighting against my faith.

Every time I go somewhere to preach a series of messages, or conduct a seminar or a convention, my natural mind always says to me, "What if nobody comes?" And then, when things start, and the people come, I always look around and think, "Wow! Just look at all these people! They really came!" That's something I have to deal with on a continual basis.

What you have to do in situations like this is that you have to get hold of yourself. Shake yourself a little bit. Remind yourself·that you're doing what God has asked you to do, and that God is so powerful that He spoke this entire universe into existence! You just can't go wrong when you're following Him.

I should also add that the Minneapolis convention was very successful — a blessing in every way to all of those who were part of it.

Now, one of the most common reasons why people give up on Plan A and start casting about for Plans B and C is that they are too impatient. They want to follow God's plan, but they want it to unfold quickly, immediately — they want it to be what I call a "microwave miracle."

They'll say, "Well, I've tried to follow the Lord's plan for my life for a week now and it doesn't seem to be working out, so I think I'll try something else."

I'm sure that this type of thinking is a result of the world we live in. We have instant coffee. Instant potatoes. Instant rice. Microwave ovens can cook in 15 minutes what used to take three or four hours. Quicker. Faster. Immediate gratification. Those are the buzzwords of modern America.

But it doesn't work that way in the realm of the spirit. Some things take time. They involve growth and perseverance. They may involve holding to a promise from God over a period of months or years!

Sarah was impatient and so she sent Abraham in to Hagar. And the result was nothing but trouble.

Abraham believed God's promise for a long, long time before he saw it come true. What we all need to do is to get to the point where we can believe and walk in the word of the Lord no matter what we see around us. Talk to yourself if you have to: "Soul, God said this, and this is the way we are going to go."

Your soul may answer you back, "Well, what about money? What about security for your family? What about...a hundred other things?" In the natural, these are all legitimate questions. But the word of the Lord is above all of that. God's ways are higher than man's ways. His thoughts are higher than man's thoughts. His plans for us are better than the plans we could devise for ourselves. (See Isaiah 55:9 and Jeremiah 29:11) So hold fast to God's Plan A for your life. Walk in it and become stable in it!

Patience is so important — not only in the realm of the spirit, but in the natural world as well. We can see the results of patience versus impatience all around us.

Some examples?

In the world of finance. One person saves and invests wisely and carefully and sees a steady growth in his net worth. The other person is always looking for a big-money, get-rich-quick scheme because he's impatient. He's always on the verge of "making it big," but never really does. That is another example of "slow and steady wins the race."

Consider, too, quick weight-loss diets. There are some diets that can help people lose weight almost overnight. But there are a lot of discouraged people walking around who lost a lot of weight in a hurry, only to see it all come back just as quickly. It takes patient, continuous dieting and exercise to keep your body in shape. There are no shortcuts. Patience and perseverance are the keys.

It takes patience to be a good parent.

It takes patience to build a strong marriage.

It takes patience to strengthen and develop your mind.

And it takes patience to wait on the Lord. But it is well worth it. As Isaiah 40:31 says:

> *"But those who wait on the Lord*
> *"Shall renew their strength;*
> *"They shall mount up with wings*
> *like eagles,*
> *"They shall run and not be weary,*
> *"They shall walk and not faint."*

40

Try not to be impatient. Don't feel that if you are waiting on the Lord, you are wasting your time. You aren't. You are gaining strength and knowledge for the task ahead of you!

Now keep in mind that patience isn't the same as inertia. I'm not talking about sitting back for months and being inactive. There is a time for patiently sitting and listening to God, and there is a time for action. When He tells you to move, move!

Here's another thing that patience is *not!* It is not sticking with the old ways of doing something when God is calling you to do something new. You see, some people have trouble keeping up with what God is doing.

One day, if the Lord tarries, the things that are occurring in the world right now will come to a divine conclusion. Something new will begin to happen, and we all need to be in tune with that, whatever it is. We need to listen to God, to be led by His Spirit, so that we are always on the cutting edge — always moving forward. God wants us to be patient and to wait on Him, but He doesn't want us to grow fat and complacent and lazy.

His job is to lead. Our job is to follow — and to hang on tenaciously to His word to us as we do.

God said to me, "Go to the nations and preach. Write books and I will sell them. Preach strong and I will draw the people.

Prophesy and you will have the ability to minister to preachers."

God gave that word to me. And as long as I hold to it and follow it, it works. If I ever hold to the operation of that word and let go of the foundation of it, I lose it. In other words, if I ever start thinking that the books I've written are really the ultimate thing, then I will lose the word of the Lord that caused them to be born and be successful. I have to hold to the word and not what the word produced.

I was in high school when the Lord first came to me and told me to write books and that He would sell them for me. Well...it's not possible to have a better literary agent than Almighty God! As long as I keep writing, trying to get the word of the Lord out to people through the printed page, I know that my books will keep on selling. Believe me when I tell you that I don't have a whole lot of time to devote to writing. But I work at it a little bit here and a little bit there, and it comes together just the way God told me it would.

Some people get mad when you live like this. They say, "I don't understand? Why does this work so well for you?" And all I can say in reply is, "I'm just following God!"

It's really that simple. God said to write the books and He would get them into the hands of those who could be blessed, encouraged and instructed by them.

I have been overseas, and had people walk

up to me and hand me a copy of one of my books in a foreign language. where I didn't even know it had been translated. And, I'll have to admit that there have been times when I thought, "Now, wait a minute. Did I sign a contract authorizing this to be done?" After all, I want to make sure everything is being done properly, you know.

But then I heard God's voice whispering to my spirit: "I didn't say anything about a contract. I just told you to write and that I would get your books into the hands of those I wanted to read them." You see, for a brief moment I was losing sight of what was important — and that is that the word of God be read by as many people as possible and that He be glorified.

And, by the grace of God, I have over a million books in print so far, in more than a dozen languages. Does that sound like bragging? Well, it's not. The success of my books is no reflection on me personally. It is a reflection of what can happen when you do what God tells you to do.

Some of you who are reading this are facing challenges and transitions in your life. You may know beyond any doubt that God spoke to you, revealing His plan for your life. You have already gone through the time of wondering, "Is this really God?" You know that it was God who spoke to you. Now is the time to hold to the word He gave you. Don't waver or doubt, but let that word be manifested in your life.

Remember the faith of Abraham. Even as he was placing Isaac on the altar, he was holding tightly to the word God had given him. He knew that even if Isaac's life were offered up in sacrifice, God could bring the boy back from the dead in order to fulfill His word that "Abraham will be the father of many nations."

You may be going through a drastic change in your life. Things aren't the way you thought they were going to be, and you don't see how they're going to change. It's easy, when this happens, to become sad, angry and frustrated, and then to let go of God's word and run back for the comfort of yesterday and the way things used to be. Don't do it! Hold on to God's word, and believe that He is able to raise your Isaac from the dead.

He can! He will!

There have been times when Isaac was dead in my life, and the only thing I had to hang on to was my faith in what God had said to me. I could only say two words: "I believe." There were times, though, when it would have been easier to say, "I quit."

But I knew I couldn't quit. I had to hang on and remind myself that God is always faithful.

There was nothing else to say or do. I couldn't talk about it. I couldn't do anything about it. I just had to believe that God's word was true and I would see, in due season, the fruit it produces.

You can have great assurance in the knowledge that God will finish whatever work He has begun in you. He will finish it, if you will hold to your faith and be persuaded that He is able to perform what He said He would do, able to fulfill every one of His promises. God wants that for you today. Hold to it! It works! God is not dead, but alive. He is all-mighty and not all-weak.

I urge you right now to find once again the word of the Lord that He has put into your heart. Don't look at your present circumstances, but find the word in your spirit. Right now, begin to pray that word. Stir it up! Keep it alive! Pray strong on that word! Let it live again!

His plans for your future are absolutely glorious! You can count on it!

Other Books by Roberts Liardon

I Saw Heaven

A Call To Action

The Invading Force

The Quest For Spiritual Hunger

The Price Of Spiritual Power

Religious Politics

Learning To Say No Without Feeling Guilty

Run to the Battle

Kathryn Kuhlman
A spiritual biography of God's miracle working power

Spiritual Timing

Breaking Controlling Powers

Cry of the Spirit
Unpublished sermons by Smith Wigglesworth

How To Survive An Attack

Haunted Houses Ghosts & Demons

Forget Not His Benefits

Holding To The Word Of The Lord

To contact Roberts Liardon
write:

Roberts Liardon Ministries
P.O. Box 30710, Laguna Hills, CA 92654

Please include your prayer requests and comments
when you write.

Additional copies of this book are available
from your local bookstore.

ALBURY PUBLISHING
P.O. Box 470406, Tulsa, OK 74137

Roberts Liardon Ministries International
Offices:

In England, Europe, Eastern Europe, and
Scandinavia

P.O. Box 2043
Hove, Brighton
East Sussex BN3 6JU

In South Africa:

Embassy Christian Centre
PO Box 2233
Kimberley 8300
South Africa